CHRISTIANITY

Published in the United States of America by Cherry Lake Publishing
Ann Arbor, Michigan
www.cherrylakepublishing.com

Content Adviser: Alexander Kocar, Princeton University

Reading Adviser: Marla Conn MS, Ed., Literacy specialist, Read-Ability, Inc.

Photo Credits: © marchello74/Shutterstock, cover, 1; © vvoe/Shutterstock, 5; © Matt Ragen/Shutterstock, 6; © Freedom Studio/Shutterstock, 8; © Renata Sedamakova/Shutterstock, 11; © Janaka Dharmasena/Shutterstock, 12; © Gerasimova Inga/Shutterstock, 14; © cdrin/Shutterstock, 16; © Rick Schroeppel/Shutterstock, 19; © giulio napolitano/Shutterstock, 21; © Peter Titmuss/Shuttterstock, 22; © Gabriel Petrescu/Shutterstock, 24; © Lisa F. Young/Shutterstock, 27; © Rawpixel.com/ Shutterstock, 28

Library of Congress Cataloging-in-Publication Data
Names: Marsico, Katie, 1980- author.
Title: Christianity / by Katie Marsico.
Description: Ann Arbor, Michigan : Cherry Lake Publishing, 2017. | Series: Global citizens: world religions |
    Includes bibliographical references and index.
Identifiers: LCCN 2016033580| ISBN 9781634721554 (hardcover) | ISBN 9781634722216 (pdf) |
    ISBN 9781634722872 (pbk.) | ISBN 9781634723534 (ebook)
Subjects: LCSH: Christianity—Juvenile literature.
Classification: LCC BR125.5 .M35 2017 | DDC 230—dc23
LC record available at https://lccn.loc.gov/2016033580

Cherry Lake Publishing would like to acknowledge the work of the Partnership for 21st Century Learning.
Please visit *www.p21.org* for more information.

Printed in the United States of America
Corporate Graphics

ABOUT THE AUTHOR

Katie Marsico is the author of more than 200 children's books. She lives in a suburb of Chicago, Illinois, with her husband and children.

TABLE OF CONTENTS

CHAPTER 1

History: Roots of the Religion

Since people began recording history, they have written about the idea of a power greater than themselves. Thousands of years later, various beliefs in God—or sometimes several gods—still shape human culture. Religion is the system people use to organize such beliefs. Religion also standardizes ceremonies and rules for worship.

A World Ruled by Romans

Christianity is one example of a major world religion. It is based on the life and teachings of Jesus of Nazareth, and what his followers (and their followers) wrote about him. Jesus was born between 6 and 4 BCE in Judaea, which formed the southern portion of ancient Palestine, the homeland of ancient Jews.

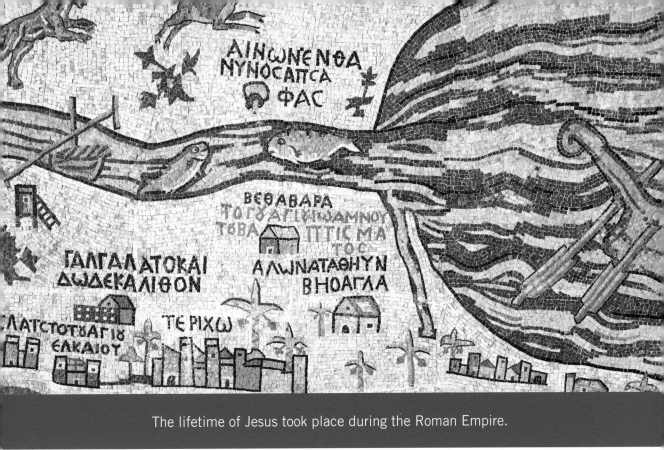

The lifetime of Jesus took place during the Roman Empire.

(Palestine is a historic region located in the Middle East, on the eastern shores of the Mediterranean Sea.)

During this period in history, Palestine was part of the Roman Empire. As a result, Roman officials controlled the area. They often relied on harsh punishments to enforce, or carry out, strict rules.

Many local residents feared the Romans. Some hated them. They prayed for the arrival of the Messiah—a special king and deliverer who God would send to save them. This belief strongly influenced the practice of Judaism, or the Jewish faith.

The Torah is written in Hebrew.

Judaism and Jesus

The ancient **Hebrews** developed Judaism about 4,000 years ago. They said there was one God, who revealed his teachings to **prophets** such as Abraham and Moses. The Hebrews also believed God's laws were found in the first five books of their scriptures, or holy writings. Together, these books were known as the Torah.

Jesus practiced Judaism and, as an adult, was frequently called rabbi. A rabbi is a teacher within the Jewish faith. By his early 30s, Jesus's teachings had become famous. His sermons, or religious speeches, often focused on the kingdom of God. He said that, within this kingdom, people had **eternal** life. In many sermons, Jesus preached about the importance of obeying God's laws and loving everyone. He also told his disciples, or followers, to ask God's forgiveness when they failed to do these things.

As time passed, incredible stories about Jesus spread throughout Palestine. His followers claimed that he performed miracles, or amazing acts. They said that he was able to heal the sick and even **resurrect** the dead!

Developing Questions

Why did Jesus's promise of eternal life appeal to his disciples? What hardships did Jews face while living in an area controlled by Roman invaders? How was Jesus's message different from what other rabbis were saying at that time?

The first question is a compelling question. The second and third are supporting questions. A compelling question doesn't have a clear answer but serves as an interesting discussion point. Supporting questions usually have more specific answers. Sometimes people use supporting questions to more closely examine compelling questions.

Jesus preached messages of forgiveness and love.

The Creation of Christianity

Some people declared that Jesus was the messiah they had been waiting for. Others thought he was a dangerous **radical**. Jewish leaders worried about Jesus's growing power. He represented a threat to their authority. Several were also concerned that the Romans would feel the same way. If they did, it was likely that they'd punish far more Jews than just Jesus.

Between 29 and 30 CE, Jewish priests had Jesus arrested. Shortly afterward, the Roman governor of Judaea ordered that

[21ST CENTURY SKILLS LIBRARY]

he be put to death. Jesus was crucified, or hung on a wooden cross to die. Later, his body was placed inside a tomb.

But Jesus's disciples said the story didn't end there. They insisted that within days, the tomb was empty. To some people, this was proof that Jesus had risen from the dead. These individuals believed that he was both human and **divine**.

As accounts of the resurrection spread, Jesus's name became more connected to the term "Christ." In Greek, the word *christos* means "**anointed** one" and is used as a translation for "messiah." The life, death, and reported resurrection of Jesus Christ led to the birth of Christianity.

Important Images

The cross is among the most widely recognized symbols used to represent Christianity. This image is a reminder of Jesus's crucifixion. Another popular Christian symbol is the ichthys, which is the outline of a fish. People believe the ichthys traces back to the fact that several of Jesus's chief disciples were fishermen. In addition, those followers who helped spread Christianity were sometimes referred to as "fishers of men."

CHAPTER 2

Geography: Mapping How Faith Formed

Christianity began in ancient Palestine. But it quickly spread to other parts of the world. Apostles, such as Paul, preached Jesus's message throughout Europe, Asia, and Africa.

At first, most of Jesus's followers were Jewish. They worked to **convert** non-Jews (**gentiles**). Within approximately 100 years of Jesus's death, most followers were now gentiles, and a new religion, Christianity, had formed. The promise of eternal life attracted followers from several different backgrounds. It didn't appeal to everyone, though. Some people misunderstood Christian **rituals** or were suspicious of the idea of miracles and resurrection.

Early Christians frequently faced persecution, or poor treatment, for their religious beliefs. Up until the fourth century,

Paul was one of the first followers of Jesus.

The New Testament of the Bible contains stories about Jesus.

many were imprisoned, tortured, and even killed. Their situation improved in 313, when the Roman emperor Constantine agreed to the Edict of Milan. This edict, or order, made it acceptable to practice Christianity, which had been illegal before. Constantine himself converted, and the Christian faith ultimately became the official religion of the Roman Empire.

Splitting and Spreading

By the early 11th century, two main branches of Christianity had formed. One was the Eastern Orthodox Church. Most people who practiced Eastern Orthodoxy spoke Greek and lived in Eastern Europe, southwestern Asia, and the Middle East. Meanwhile, Christians in Western Europe generally belonged to the Roman Catholic Church. Latin was the official language used in Roman Catholicism.

Gathering and Evaluating Sources

What's the best place to find stories about Jesus's life, death, and resurrection? Christians view the first four books of the New Testament, or gospels, as valuable sources of information. (The New Testament is the second part of the Christian Bible. The Old Testament is the first part. It contains scripture describing the religious experiences of the ancient Hebrews.)

There are four gospel authors, or evangelists—Matthew, Mark, Luke, and John. Many Christians believe Matthew and John were Jesus's apostles. The evangelists probably wrote the gospels between 70 and 95 CE. Some people have pointed out that there are slight differences in their accounts. But it's likely these men were more concerned about spreading Christianity than presenting historical facts.

CHRISTIANITY

THE GLOBAL DISTRIBUTION OF CHRISTIANS

†††††††††††††††††† AUSTRALIA AND OCEANIA 24 MILLION
†††††††††††††††††† CANADA 25 MILLION
†††††††††††††††††† USA 160–225 MILLION
†††††††††††††††††† NORTH AMERICA 231 MILLION
†††††††††††††††††† ASIA 356 MILLION
†††††††††††††††††† AFRICA 475 MILLION
†††††††††††††††††† LATIN AMERICA 543 MILLION
†††††††††††††††††† EUROPE 400–550 MILLION

Today, Christianity is practiced all over the world.

Differences in culture, politics, and specific beliefs all led to the creation of these separate denominations, or religious subgroups. During the next several hundred years, Christianity split into other branches for similar reasons. Eastern Orthodoxy, Roman Catholicism, and Protestantism—which developed in 16th-century Western Europe—are the three major Christian denominations. There are many additional subgroups, though. Altogether, roughly 41,000 Christian denominations exist worldwide!

[21ST CENTURY SKILLS LIBRARY]

Wide-Reaching Religious Beliefs

Since the 11th century, Christianity has spread to every continent on Earth. European **missionaries** introduced this religion to several parts of Asia, Africa, North America, and South America. Sometimes people in these areas were eager to convert to Christianity. In other cases, they were forced to change religions when European soldiers invaded their homelands.

Hoping to Regain Holy Lands

Between the 11th and 13th centuries, European Christians became involved in the Crusades. During these holy wars, people who practiced Christianity battled Muslims. (Muslims are members of the Islamic faith.) Christians hoped to regain the Holy Land in what had once been ancient Palestine. Areas that made up the Holy Land served as the setting of many biblical events, including Jesus's crucifixion. For the most part, European crusaders proved unsuccessful.

This parade in San Miguel de Allende, Mexico, celebrates Good Friday every year.

Today, researchers say that almost 2.2 billion Christians represent nearly one-third of the world's population! This makes Christianity the most widely practiced religion. More than 11 percent of the world's Christians live in the United States. Approximately a quarter of the Christian population is found in Brazil, Mexico, Russia, and the Philippines. Nigeria, China, Democratic Republic of the Congo, Germany, and Ethiopia are also home to large numbers of Christians.

According to recent studies, half of all Christians are Roman Catholic. About 37 percent are Protestant, and roughly 12 percent are Eastern Orthodox. A small amount of Christians belong to denominations that aren't grouped within these three main branches.

CHAPTER 3

Civics: Organization and Ideas

Most Christian denominations share certain common beliefs. For starters, Jesus is considered the divine son of God and a member of the Holy Trinity. The Holy Trinity is based on the idea that God is actually three beings. These are the Father, the Son (Jesus), and the **Holy Spirit**, which is often represented as a dove.

All Christians also rely on biblical accounts of Jesus's teachings to support their faith. They think that before Jesus died, the sins people committed separated them from God. His death was a **sacrifice** that helped human beings achieve forgiveness. In turn, God was able to welcome them into his kingdom, where they experience eternal life. An important idea within Christianity is that the souls, or spirits, of the faithful never die. Instead, they live on forever, even after a person's body no longer exists.

Christians believe Jesus came back to life, after his painful death on the cross.

Christians say that, following the resurrection, Jesus spent time among his disciples. Eventually, however, he joined God the Father in heaven. Still, many Christians are confident that Jesus will one day return to Earth. At that point, a final judgment will occur. Jesus will decide who has been faithful and who is truly sorry for their sins. The souls of those people will then enter God's kingdom.

Roman Catholicism

Despite their common roots, different Christian denominations have different features. For example, the Roman

Catholic Church is not organized in the same way as the Protestant or Eastern Orthodox churches. Roman Catholics consider the pope—who lives in Rome—to be the leader of their faith. Other Roman Catholic **clergy** include cardinals, archbishops, bishops, priests, and deacons. These ministers are all male. Most are never allowed to marry because they are said to already be married to the church.

In Roman Catholicism, clergy act as mediators, or middlemen, who help people become closer to God. They oversee the celebration of mass and **sacraments** such as baptism and **reconciliation**. Many Roman Catholics view these religious **rites** as ways to achieve love, guidance, and grace, or

Developing Claims and Using Evidence

What led some Europeans to split from the Roman Catholic Church and begin the Protestant movement in the 1500s? As you develop an answer to this question, consider the differences between Roman Catholicism and Protestantism. Be sure to also use other sources of information to support your ideas. Visit the library, head online, or talk to an adult about contacting local churches! (Hint: Not all Internet sources are always reliable. Web sites operated by government organizations or colleges and universities are usually good places to start!)

Pope Francis has been leading the Catholic Church since 2013.

God's favor. They are traditions that—along with the Bible—guide Christians who practice Roman Catholicism.

Roman Catholics also have an extremely deep respect for the **saints** and Jesus's mother, Mary. They frequently pray *through* these figures. Members of the Roman Catholic Church believe that Mary and the saints are able to reach out and speak to God on their behalf.

Protestantism

Unlike Roman Catholics, Protestants don't view the pope as the leader of their faith. Clergy within this branch of Christianity

Protestant churches allow women to lead.

includes pastors, ministers, reverends, elders, and deacons. Not all Protestant clergy are men, and some are allowed to marry.

Protestants look to clergy for guidance and support—not mediation between themselves and God. They believe all people are able to build their own relationship with God and communicate with him directly. Most Protestants also think of sacraments as symbols of grace, versus opportunities to achieve it. Finally, members of Protestant churches respect Mary and the saints, but normally don't pray through them.

[21ST CENTURY SKILLS LIBRARY]

Eastern Orthodoxy

Within the Eastern Orthodox Church, the clergy is made up of various types of bishops, priests, and deacons. There is no central figure such as a pope leading these individuals. To members of the Eastern Orthodox Church, the pope is simply one of many patriarchs, or senior bishops.

Patriarchs oversee individual territories where Eastern Orthodoxy is practiced. Each patriarch has headquarters in a holy city such as Rome or Jerusalem. (Jerusalem is now the

Bread and Wine, Body and Blood

Faith often involves believing in miracles without having physical evidence to prove they occurred. This is how some Christians accept the miracle of transubstantiation. They say transubstantiation is the process by which a blessing changes bread and wine into the Eucharist, or communion. People who receive the Eucharist believe they are partaking of Jesus's body and blood. Transubstantiation re-creates the final supper Jesus shared with his apostles the night before his crucifixion. Based on sight alone, the Eucharist looks like bread and wine. For many Christians, however, it is far more.

These men are clergy in the Eastern Orthodox Church.

capital of Israel. It used to be part of ancient Palestine and is where Jesus was crucified.) The majority of Eastern Orthodox clergy are male, and some are married.

In many ways, the Eastern Orthodox Church is quite similar to the Roman Catholic Church. One difference is that they don't use the same calendar system. The Eastern Orthodox Church sets holidays based on the Julian calendar. In contrast, Roman Catholics and Protestants rely on the Gregorian calendar. This means Christmas and Easter—which celebrate Jesus's birth and resurrection—fall on different dates in Eastern Orthodoxy.

Celebrating Faith

In Christianity, several holidays and festivals serve as opportunities for people to celebrate their beliefs. Some of the main Christian holidays are described below.

Holiday	When It's Celebrated	Main Theme
Advent	November and December	The beginning of the Christian year, a time when people prepare to celebrate the birth of Jesus
Christmas	Late December or early January	Celebration that focuses on the birth of Jesus
Lent	Late winter or early spring	Season of prayer and sacrifice (giving up certain foods and pleasurable activities) that begins 40 days before Easter and recalls Jesus's suffering
Easter	Spring	Celebration that recalls Jesus's resurrection
All Saints' Day	Varies	Celebration when Christians remember the lives and works of all their saints
Note: Dates often vary, depending on the geographic location of individual faith communities and the practices within different denominations.		

CHAPTER 4

Economics: Funding a Faith

All religions—including Christianity—rely on faith to survive. But they depend on economic support, too. It costs money to build and care for property such as churches, religious offices, and housing where clergy live. Funding also pays for staff who oversee church finances, religious education, and community **outreach**. It's not uncommon for churches to offer relief to people who are struggling with poverty. Some use their funding to operate pantries that provide free food to the hungry. Others support shelters that give the homeless a place to sleep for the night.

Christian churches also need money to fund mission trips. Missionaries teach people about Jesus and invite them to make Christianity their faith. In addition, they often work with communities to improve local schools, housing, and health care.

Many people donate money to the church where they attend services.

Various Means of Earning Money

Most Christian churches get much of their funding from their own members. Sometimes these individuals simply give what they're able to afford. Others tithe, or set aside 10 percent of their earnings as an offering. Some people leave the church money in their **will**. Several Christian churches also raise funds by renting out their facilities or meeting spaces.

Christianity has millions of supporters all over the world.

Communicating Conclusions

Think about why it's important for Christian churches to fund community outreach. Find out what types of programming such churches support in your area. Select the program that interests you the most and research it further. Next, list all the ways it helps people. Predict how these individuals' lives would change if the program you picked lost church funding. Discuss your conclusions with friends, family, and other members of your community!

[21ST CENTURY SKILLS LIBRARY]

A Powerful Presence

With the help of its members, Christianity remains one of the world's best-known and most widespread religions. Its global reach is based on shared beliefs about Jesus. At the same time, different Christian denominations are influenced by many unique ideas. The incredible history of this religion continues to shape the faith of Christians today. As a result, Christianity is likely to remain a powerful presence well into the future.

Taking Informed Action

Today, people around the world—including Christians—continue to face persecution for their faith. Do your part to end this intolerance, or lack of acceptance! Start by helping raise awareness about Christianity and other religions. One idea is to create a chart by dividing a piece of paper into three to five columns. At the top of each column, write the name of a major world religion. (Christianity, Buddhism, Hinduism, Islam, Sikhism, and Judaism are a few possibilities.) Within each column, list brief descriptions of that religion's beliefs and traditions. Highlight any shared features that appear in more than one column. If you practice a certain religion, show your chart to members of your own faith community.

Think About It

A recent study by the Pew Research Center (PRC) revealed some interesting statistics comparing Christianity of the past and present. (PRC research provides the public with data on important issues both within the United States and around the world.) The PRC examined how many Christians make up the world's population today versus roughly a century ago. Currently, Christians form about 32 percent of the world's population. This number is only slightly less than what it was in the early 20th century. At that point, Christians represented approximately 35 percent of the world's population.

PRC researchers also determined that the European Christian population has decreased by 19 percent. Meanwhile, the American Christian population is down by 10 percent (compared to what it was about a century ago). What are you able to conclude from these statistics? (Hint: During the past century, how have Christian populations changed in areas besides Europe, North America, and South America?)

For More Information

FURTHER READING

Glossop, Jennifer, and John Mantha (illustrator). *The Kids Book of World Religions.* Toronto: Kids Can Press, Ltd., 2013.

Osborne, Mary Pope, and Michael Welpy (illustrator). *The Random House Book of Bible Stories.* New York City: Random House Books for Young Readers, 2009.

WEB SITES

Social Studies for Kids—Christianity
www.socialstudiesforkids.com/subjects/christianity.htm
Head here for links to multiple kid-friendly sites that provide further information about Christianity.

United Religions Initiative—Kids: Christianity
www.uri.org/kids/world_chri.htm
Visit this site to learn more about Christian beliefs, celebrations, and sacred spaces.

GLOSSARY

anointed (uh-NOINT-ed) chosen by divine election

clergy (KLUR-jee) a group of people trained to lead religious groups, such as priests, ministers, and rabbis

convert (kuhn-VERT) change one's religious beliefs

divine (dih-VINE) having to do with God

eternal (ih-TUR-nuhl) lasting or staying the same forever

gentiles (JEN-tiles) people who are not Jewish

Hebrews (HEE-brooz) members of, or descendants from, one of the Jewish tribes of ancient times

Holy Spirit (HOH-lee SPIR-it) one of the three beings of the Christian Trinity

missionaries (MISH-uh-ner-eez) people sent to a foreign country to teach about religion and do good works

outreach (OUT-reech) the extending of services or assistance

prophets (PRAH-fits) people who speak or claim to speak to God

radical (RAD-i-kuhl) a person in favor of extreme changes in existing views or conditions

reconciliation (rek-uhn-sil-ee-AY-shuhn) making up after a disagreement

resurrect (rez-ur-EKT) to bring a dead person back to life

rites (RITES) acts that are part of a religious ceremony

rituals (RICH-oo-uhlz) acts that are always performed in the same way, usually as part of a religious or social ceremony

sacraments (SAK-ruh-ments) important Christian ceremonies (such as baptism or marriage)

sacrifice (SAK-ruh-fise) the offering of something to God or a god

saints (SAYNTZ) in certain Christian churches, people who have been officially recognized for having lived very holy lives

will (WIL) a legal document that contains instructions stating what should happen to someone's property and money when the person dies

INDEX